Help! I've Got an Alarm Bell Going Off in My Head!

The Panicosaurus
Managing Anxiety in Children Including
Those with Asperger Syndrome
K.I. Al-Ghani
Illustrated by Haitham Al-Ghani
ISBN 978 1 84905 356 3
eISBN 978 0 85700 706 3

Can I tell you about Anxiety?
A guide for friends, family and professionals
Lucy Willetts and Polly Waite
Illustrated by Kaiyee Tay
ISBN 978 1 84905 527 7
eISBN 978 0 85700 967 8

Frankie's Foibles
A story about a boy who worries
Kath Grimshaw
ISBN 978 1 84905 695 3
eISBN 978 1 78450 210 2

Help!

I've Got an Alarm Bell Going Off in My Head!

How Panic, Anxiety and Stress Affect Your Body

K.L. Aspden
Foreword by Babette Rothschild
Illustrated by Zíta Rá

Jessica Kingsley *Publishers*
London and Philadelphia

First published in 2016
by Jessica Kingsley Publishers
73 Collier Street
London N1 9BE, UK
and
400 Market Street, Suite 400
Philadelphia, PA 19106, USA

www.jkp.com

Library of Congress Cataloging in Publication Data
Aspden, K. L.
Help - I've got an alarm bell going off in my head! : how panic, anxiety and stress affect
your body / K.L.
Aspden ; foreword by Babette Rothschild.
pages cm
Audience: Ages 9-11.
ISBN 978-1-84905-704-2 (alk. paper)
1. Panic attacks--Juvenile literature. 2. Anxiety disorders--Juvenile literature. I. Title.
RC535.A87 2016
616.85'223--dc23
2015029309

British Library Cataloguing in Publication Data
A CIP catalogue record for this book is available from the British Library

ISBN 978 1 84905 704 2
eISBN 978 1 78450 227 0

Printed and bound in Great Britain by Bell and Bain Ltd, Glasgow

MIX
Paper from
responsible sources
FSC
www.fsc.org   FSC® C007785

This book is dedicated to the children I have worked with, who have had the courage to share their struggles and have taught me so much.

Contents

Foreword

The brain and nervous system's alarm process, which helps us to recognise and survive danger, is fantastic. It saves lives. Literally. When signs of threat emerge, the middle part of the brain (called the limbic system) activates the body to flee or fight. If neither of those is possible it makes the body immobile by making the muscles freeze. Stress hormones are released to meet these survival demands. At the same time, these same hormones ensure the thinking part of the brain (the cortex) is held back. When life is threatened, immediate and quick responses are necessary for survival. Thinking would slow down reaction times and put survival at risk. Most of the time, once the danger has passed this alarm is silenced and normal life resumes. However, there are plenty of instances where, for various reasons, the brain and nervous system do not get (or understand) the message that the danger has passed. In those cases, an alarm continues to sound and difficulty in daily life results. K.L. Aspden's marvellous book is a wonderful contribution to helping people of all ages who are suffering from the continuous sounding of this survival alarm. With solid information, good humour, engaging cartoons and helpful suggestions, this small book speaks volumes about helping young and old to heal from trauma.

Babette Rothschild, author of
The Body Remembers: The Psychophysiology of Trauma *and*
Trauma Treatment and 8 Keys to Safe Trauma Recovery

Introduction

If you have strong reactions that you don't understand, this book is written for you. If you know or work with someone who struggles with anxiety, this book is written for you. It may help you discover that there are reasons behind these difficulties. It may help you discover ways to reduce the distress caused by these experiences.

This book is intended to be read bit by bit and talked about with someone.

It will be most helpful if you try out and practise the ideas as much as you can.

1

The Alarm

We all have an **alarm bell** in our head, like a fire alarm, to keep us safe in emergencies.

We all have an alarm bell in our
head, like a fire alarm...

Its posh name is the **amygdala** (*am-ig-dulla*), and it is found in our brain. When we are in danger, it sends off a loud signal to our body.

...to run for it...

...fight for our lives...

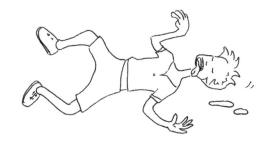

...or pretend to be dead...

It is a very clever system when it is working properly. Our brain sends messages down to our adrenal glands, which sit on top of our kidneys. They pump out large amounts of adrenalin (a specially designed chemical) to prepare us for action. Blood rushes to our arms and legs, our heart races and we are ready to escape the danger. This all happens in a split second.

Our thinking is automatically turned off so that it doesn't get in the way. There's no time for that!

Our thinking is automatically turned off...

The only problem is that the *amygdala* sometimes starts going off at all the wrong times, when there is no emergency. You could describe it as a 'false alarm'. This can feel terrible for the person it happens to. If it happens to you, you will recognise some of these feelings:

...shaking...

...anger...

...crying...

...frozen to the spot...

...dry mouth,
sweaty hands...

...wobbliness...

...surge
of energy...

...aggression, maybe
kicking, punching,
swearing...

...dizziness...

...shutting down, feeling
far away or like you
are disappearing...

If your alarm goes off you will certainly not be able to think clearly. The only thoughts will be about **running away** or **fighting**, or that **something dreadful** is about to happen. These **unhelpful thoughts** keep the alarm going, and keep all the adrenalin pumping around your body.

2

Switching On

The situations that switch on the alarm are different for each of us. These situations are called **triggers**; some people describe triggers as situations that are **'pressing your buttons'**.

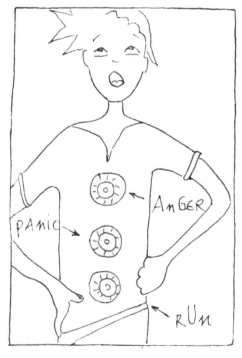

'pressing your buttons'

These triggers can come from outside or inside of us and make us feel like we are in danger even when we are not.

An **outside trigger** may be something that happens, like an unexpected loud noise, a thunderstorm, someone calling you names, or even a smell.

An **inside trigger** could be a feeling you have in your body, or a thought you have in your mind. *This can feel just as scary and can be hard to notice.*

If you find that your alarm keeps going off accidentally, then it will be very useful to find out what is triggering it.

Here are some common triggers:

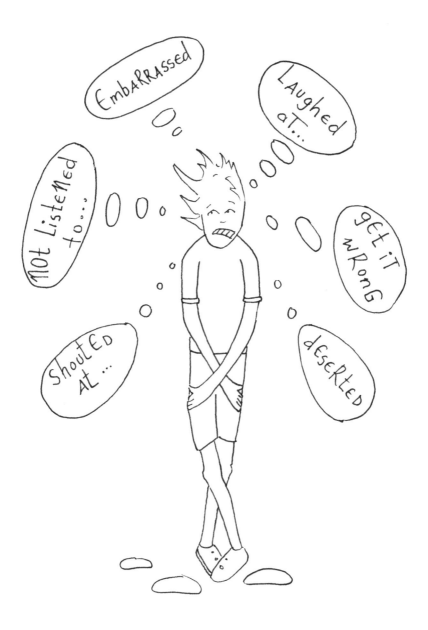

Common triggers...

There are hundreds more and most of them involve **fear**. Think about your own fears – we all have them! If you know yourself well, then you will be more prepared when you have a **false alarm**.

Why not try writing down some of your triggers?

If you have lots of triggers and your alarm keeps going off, here is an important message:

Some people have an alarm system that switches on easily. This can be because difficult things have happened in their lives. Our body holds memories about everything, even the things we can't remember because we were very young when they happened. If we have had a lot of danger around us then our body will always be on red alert, waiting for the next bad thing to happen. The alarm will be ready to go off at any moment.

It can also be this way for many people who have autism, Asperger's syndrome and ADHD. The world can be too busy, scary and confusing.

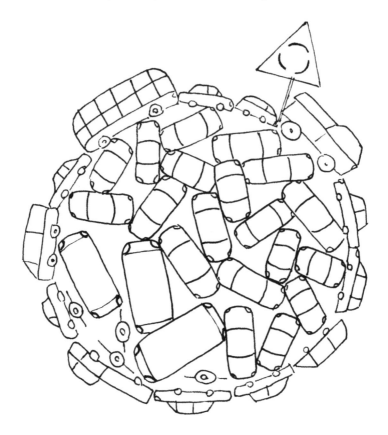

The world can be...confusing.

Everybody has false alarms at times. If you feel this way, you are not the only one.

And **you are not to blame** if your amygdala is over-active. It just needs a bit of help.

3

Switching Off

There is good news – we can learn to **switch off the alarm!** There are lots of things that can help us to do this. They are simple ideas but they are *not necessarily easy*.

Helping our amygdala is like training a lively dog who is determined to protect his owner.

Helping our amygdala is like training a lively dog...

Dogs take time to learn new tricks; the trainer and the dog both need to keep practising! Sometimes we need support with training our amydgala from someone who understands – maybe a friend, your mum or dad, a teacher or a counsellor.

Ideas to try

You could practise these ideas with someone you trust.

1. **Remember that your reaction is a false alarm.** Your body needs to be reminded of this.

   - *Make a reminder notice or draw a picture and put it on your wall.*

   - *Carry something in your pocket as a reminder.*

   - *Put a message in your phone.*

Make yourself 'reminders'...

2. **Breathe.** It works if you take some slower breaths. This will be the last thing your body wants to do, but it will calm things down.

- *Take a breath as you count to six in your head. Breathe out as you count to eight.*
                                    (Repeat a few times)

- *Take a breath and notice the air coming in and out of your body.*
                            (Repeat six or more times)

Take some slower breaths...

3. **Turn your thinking back on** by doing something simple.

- *Count things.*

- *Name objects that begin with the same letter.*

- *Spell your name backwards!*

- *Think of the words of a favourite song.*

(Can you think of some other ideas? Write them down now while you are not in a panic.)

4. Make yourself feel solid again.

- *Feel the ground under your feet.*

- *Slap or rub your arms.*

- *Gently push against something firm.*

- *Touch something soft and something hard, something warm and something cold.*

Touch something solid...

5. **Come back to now** by noticing what is around you.

- *The colour of the carpet.*

- *The feel of your jumper.*

- *The temperature of your hands.*

- *A picture on the wall.*

6. Concentrate on something that makes you feel happy or peaceful, or that makes you laugh. You will need to think about this in advance so that you are prepared.

- Your *favourite animal – carry a picture with you.*

- *A peaceful place – keep a photo nearby to remind you.*

- *A piece of music you love – if you can, have it with you.*

Concentrate on something that
makes you feel happy...

7. **Talk to someone** who will listen. Being heard is very calming. Talk to someone as soon as you begin to feel that things are getting difficult. It is better to do this before the pressure builds up inside you.

4

Looking After the Alarm System

Some things will not change. We may not be able to stop our false alarms altogether, but we can help ourselves a lot by doing things that are **calming**.

The plan here is to keep the stress chemicals, like adrenalin, at a low level. When they build up inside us, we feel on edge and very uncomfortable – our alarm system will be triggered much more easily.

It will help if you remember that human beings have **three possible danger zones**.

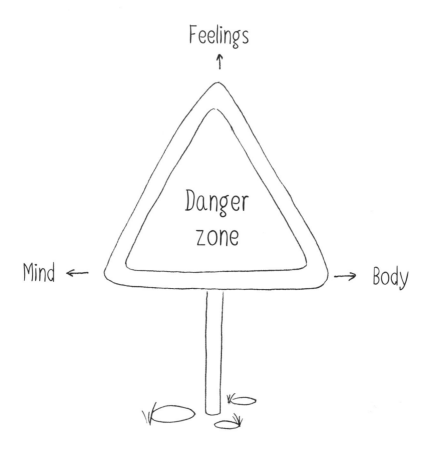

If you feel a bit wobbly or 'not quite yourself', it is a good idea to carry out an **alarm system patrol** – check out the three danger zones to find out what is happening.

Alarm system patrol

If you discover trouble in any of these zones, then it is likely that your amygdala is on the look out for emergencies and your false alarm could be getting ready to go off. By noticing what is going on you can take more control.

Danger Zone One: Your mind

Notice what you are thinking...

The 'what ifs' are especially dangerous!

Danger Zone Two: Your feelings

Are you angry, lonely or worried...

. . .or maybe excited or scared?

Danger Zone Three: Your body

Do you feel tired, hungry or poorly...

...or is something hurting?

If you can find out what the problem is, then you have carried out excellent detective work! It is an achievement because it means you can ask for help before those stress chemicals send your alarm system 'bananas'.

To keep things peaceful...

Try out these top tips yourself.

For your mind

Use your imagination to help you. Think of a real memory that gives you fabulous feelings – maybe baking a cake, or a trip to the beach. Picture the scene in your mind and sense the feelings in your body. When your thoughts are causing problems you can take yourself to that place in your head.

...imagine baking a cake...

For your feelings

My number one tip for difficult feelings is to **do something creative**. This puts your emotions outside of your body. Examples are writing, playing an instrument, drawing, or making something that shows how you feel. These activities are especially good if you can't find the right words, as they don't have to make any sense.

...play an instrument...

For your body

Exercise gives your body different chemicals that make you feel **positive** and **uplifted**. It also helps to get rid of adrenalin. Try doing something you enjoy – perhaps go for a bike ride or play football.

...perhaps go for a bike ride or play football...

Some people find it calming to concentrate on their body, starting with their feet and slowly going all the way up to their heads. This is called a **body scan** and can be really helpful if you can't get to sleep.

There are *many* more things you could try to help your amygdala stay calm. There isn't room here to write about them all; in fact, there are probably more ideas than there are people on this planet! When you have finished this book maybe you could make a list of things that help *you* to feel **peaceful** and **happy**.

...feel peaceful and happy.

Thank You

Thank you to all my friends and family who have believed in me.

I am especially grateful to those who have supported me throughout the process of delivering my ideas into these pages. Thank you to Jenny and Arthur Dickson for your friendship and ongoing commitment to all my creative projects, to Carol Hyatt for hours spent checking details and providing technical help, to Liz Woolf for understanding how it is to create something from the depths of experience, to Mary Smail, who taught me to trust my intuition, and to Theresa McCann who has cheered me on all the way.

I also want to thank Zita Rà, who has brought my words to life with her fantastic illustrations, Babette Rothschild for kindly contributing the foreword, and the staff at Jessica Kingsley Publishers.